The Story of Jesus and the Apostles, for children

The Twelve Ordinary Men

Matthew 4:18–22; 9:9; 14:22–23; 26:36–44 and 27:3–5;
Mark 1:16–20; Luke 5:1–11 and 6:12–16;
John 1:35–51; 6:7; 19:25–27 and 20:24–29

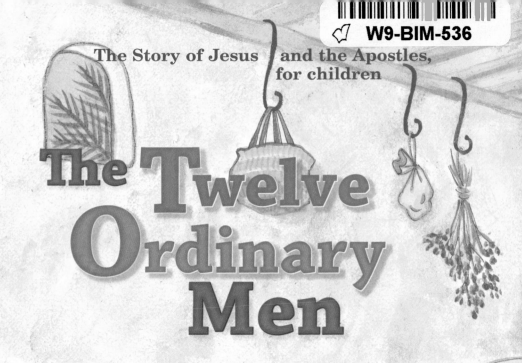

Written by Kelly Skipworth
Illustrated by Chris Wold Dyrud

CONCORDIA PUBLISHING HOUSE • SAINT LOUIS

Jesus called twelve ordinary men
To leave their homes and follow Him.
Who were these men who took the call?
True heroes of the faith, all!

Peter was a fisherman;
His brother Andrew fished with him,
'Til one day, Jesus said to them,
"Now come with Me and fish for men."

Andrew watched most nervously
As Peter stepped out on the sea.
When Peter sank quite suddenly,
The Lord said, "Peter, just trust in Me!"

James and John were brothers too—
They followed Christ, and their faith grew.
Called "Sons of Thunder," they were loud,
And Zebedee, their dad, was proud.

John stood crying at the cross
And felt for Mary's awful loss.
Before He died, the Lord said, "John,
She'll be your mother when I'm gone."

Peter, James and John—these three—
They prayed with Christ at Gethsemane.
Though Jesus had no time to lose,
The three men took some time to snooze!

When the crowd was low on bread,
The price tag danced in Philip's head.
"It'll cost a fortune," Philip said,
"To make sure all these mouths get fed."

Philip went to tell his friend
About the Christ that God did send.
Nathanael sat beneath a tree
'Til Philip said, "Please, come and see!"

Matthew was a publican—
A tax collector—that's no fun!
But he was richer than the rest
And gave up more to leave the nest.

James the Less was likely small.
The Bible has his name—that's all.
But like the others, he gave all,
And he was faithful to the call.

One disciple's claim to fame
Was having three distinctive names.
Perhaps best known as Thaddaeus,
But Judas, too, and Lebbaeus.

Simon thought that he'd been sent
To fight the Roman government.
This zealot put away his sword
When he was called by our Lord.

Judas earned some coins for this:
Betraying Jesus with a kiss.
He hanged himself upon a tree—
So sad that he'd made history!

Doubting Thomas shook his head
When he heard Jesus was not dead.
He needed proof, and so he cried,
"I need to feel His hands and side!"

Heroes of the Bible, true—
The Christian Church began with few.
The Gospel then was boldly shared—
All thanks to these first men who dared!

Dear Parents,

Everywhere Jesus went, people gathered to hear Him preach and teach. He had many disciples—people who were called to trust in Him as their Savior and who told others about Him. But Jesus chose twelve disciples, the apostles, for a special purpose.

For three years, these men traveled with Jesus, eyewitnesses to all of His works. He taught them about the kingdom of God through parables and sermons and conversations. After His resurrection, Jesus gave the apostles what we call the Great Commission, the task of establishing the Christian Church by teaching and baptizing in the name of the Triune God (Matthew 28:18–19). He sent the Holy Spirit to the apostles, and bestowed upon them His very authority and power (John 20:22–23).

For the rest of their lives, they preached, baptized, performed miracles, and recorded Jesus' teachings and their own acts in His name. The Christian Church is built on their work. And to this day, we continue to follow their example by confessing our faith in Jesus Christ, our Lord and Savior from sin, and by declaring the wonders of God, who has "called us out of darkness into His marvelous light" (1 Peter 2:9).

The Editor